Children in Exile

BY JAMES FENTON

Terminal Moraine (1972)
You Were Marvellous (1983)
Children in Exile: Poems 1968–1984 (1984)
Partingtime Hall (with John Fuller, 1987)
All the Wrong Places: Adrift in the Politics of the Pacific Rim (1988)
Out of Danger (1994)

Children in Exile
Poems 1968-1984

James Fenton

THE NOONDAY PRESS
FARRAR STRAUS GIROUX
New York

Originally published in Great Britain as *The Memory of War* and
Children in Exile by The Salamander Press, Edinburgh, in 1982 and
1983. Originally published in North America by Random House,
Inc., in 1984
First Noonday Press edition, 1994

LIBRARY OF CONGRESS CATALOGING-IN-PUBLICATION DATA
Fenton, James.
Children in exile : poems, 1968–1984 / James Fenton.—1st
noonday ed.
p.   cm.
I. Title.
PR6056.E53A6   1994
821'.914—dc20   93-40177 CIP

Contents

I

A German Requiem

(To T. J. G.-A.)

For as at a great distance of place, that which wee look at, appears dimme, and without distinction of the smaller parts; and as Voyces grow weak, and inarticulate: so also after great distance of time, our imagination of the Past is weak; and wee lose (for example) of Cities wee have seen, many particular Streets; and of Actions, many particular Circumstances. This *decaying sense*, when wee would express the thing it self, (I mean *fancy* it selfe,) wee call *Imagination*, as I said before: But when we would express the *decay*, and signifie that the Sense is fading, old, and past, it is called Memory. So that *Imagination* and *Memory* are but one thing . . .

Hobbes, *Leviathan*

A German Requiem

It is not what they built. It is what they knocked down.
It is not the houses. It is the spaces between the houses.
It is not the streets that exist. It is the streets that no longer exist.
It is not your memories which haunt you.
It is not what you have written down.
It is what you have forgotten, what you must forget.
What you must go on forgetting all your life.
And with any luck oblivion should discover a ritual.
You will find out that you are not alone in the enterprise.
Yesterday the very furniture seemed to reproach you.
Today you take your place in the Widow's Shuttle.

¶

The bus is waiting at the southern gate
To take you to the city of your ancestors
Which stands on the hill opposite, with gleaming pediments,
As vivid as this charming square, your home.
Are you shy? You should be. It is almost like a wedding,
The way you clasp your flowers and give a little tug at your veil. Oh,
The hideous bridesmaids, it is natural that you should resent them
Just a little, on this first day.
But that will pass, and the cemetery is not far.
Here comes the driver, flicking a toothpick into the gutter,
His tongue still searching between his teeth.
See, he has not noticed you. No one has noticed you.
It will pass, young lady, it will pass.

¶

How comforting it is, once or twice a year,
To get together and forget the old times.
As on those special days, ladies and gentlemen,
When the boiled shirts gather at the graveside
And a leering waistcoat approaches the rostrum.
It is like a solemn pact between the survivors.
The mayor has signed it on behalf of the freemasonry.
The priest has sealed it on behalf of all the rest.
Nothing more need be said, and it is better that way—

¶

The better for the widow, that she should not live in fear of surprise,
The better for the young man, that he should move at liberty between
   the armchairs,
The better that these bent figures who flutter among the graves
Tending the nightlights and replacing the chrysanthemums
Are not ghosts,
That they shall go home.
The bus is waiting, and on the upper terraces
The workmen are dismantling the houses of the dead.

¶

But when so many had died, so many and at such speed,
There were no cities waiting for the victims.
They unscrewed the name-plates from the shattered doorways
And carried them away with the coffins.
So the squares and parks were filled with the eloquence of young
  cemeteries :
The smell of fresh earth, the improvised crosses
And all the impossible directions in brass and enamel.

¶

'Doctor Gliedschirm, skin specialist, surgeries 14-16 hours or by
    appointment.'
Professor Sargnagel was buried with four degrees, two associate
    memberships
And instructions to tradesmen to use the back entrance.
Your uncle's grave informed you that he lived on the third floor, left.
You were asked please to ring, and he would come down in the lift
To which one needed a key . . .

¶

Would come down, would ever come down
With a smile like thin gruel, and never too much to say.
How he shrank through the years.
How you towered over him in the narrow cage.
How he shrinks now . . .

¶

But come. Grief must have its term? Guilt too, then.
And it seems there is no limit to the resourcefulness of recollection.
So that a man might say and think :
When the world was at its darkest,
When the black wings passed over the rooftops
(And who can divine His purposes?) even then
There was always, always a fire in this hearth.
You see this cupboard? A priest-hole !
And in that lumber-room whole generations have been housed and fed.
Oh, if I were to begin, if I were to begin to tell you
The half, the quarter, a mere smattering of what we went through !

¶

His wife nods, and a secret smile,
Like a breeze with enough strength to carry one dry leaf
Over two pavingstones, passes from chair to chair.
Even the enquirer is charmed.
He forgets to pursue the point.
It is not what he wants to know.
It is what he wants not to know.
It is not what they say.
It is what they do not say.

II

Cambodia

One man shall smile one day and say goodbye.
Two shall be left, two shall be left to die.

One man shall give his best advice.
Three men shall pay the price.

One man shall live, live to regret.
Four men shall meet the debt.

One man shall wake from terror to his bed.
Five men shall be dead.

One man to five. A million men to one.
And still they die. And still the war goes on.

In a Notebook

There was a river overhung with trees
With wooden houses built along its shallows
From which the morning sun drew up a haze
And the gyrations of the early swallows
Paid no attention to the gentle breeze
Which spoke discreetly from the weeping willows.
There was a jetty by the forest clearing
Where a small boat was tugging at its mooring.

And night still lingered underneath the eaves.
In the dark houseboats families were stirring
And Chinese soup was cooked on charcoal stoves.
Then one by one there came into the clearing
Mothers and daughters bowed beneath their sheaves.
The silent children gathered round me staring
And the shy soldiers setting out for battle
Asked for a cigarette and laughed a little.

From low canoes old men laid out their nets
While on the bank young boys with lines were fishing.
The wicker traps were drawn up by their floats.
The girls stood waist-deep in the river washing
Or tossed the day's rice on enamel plates
And I sat drinking bitter coffee wishing
The tide would turn to bring me to my senses
After the pleasant war and the evasive answers.

There was a river overhung with trees.
The girls stood waist-deep in the river washing,
And night still lingered underneath the eaves
While on the bank young boys with lines were fishing.
Mothers and daughters bowed beneath their sheaves
While I sat drinking bitter coffee wishing –
And the tide turned and brought me to my senses.
The pleasant war brought the unpleasant answers.

The villages are burnt, the cities void;
The morning light has left the river view;
The distant followers have been dismayed;
And I'm afraid, reading this passage now,
That everything I knew has been destroyed
By those whom I admired but never knew;
The laughing soldiers fought to their defeat
And I'm afraid most of my friends are dead.

Dead Soldiers

When His Excellency Prince Norodom Chantaraingsey
Invited me to lunch on the battlefield
I was glad of my white suit for the first time that day.
They lived well, the mad Norodoms, they had style.
The brandy and the soda arrived in crates.
Bricks of ice, tied around with raffia,
Dripped from the orderlies' handlebars.

And I remember the dazzling tablecloth
As the APCs fanned out along the road,
The dishes piled high with frogs' legs,
Pregnant turtles, their eggs boiled in the carapace,
Marsh irises in fish sauce
And inflorescence of a banana salad.

On every bottle, Napoleon Bonaparte
Pleaded for the authenticity of the spirit.
They called the empties Dead Soldiers
And rejoiced to see them pile up at our feet.

Each diner was attended by one of the other ranks
Whirling a table-napkin to keep off the flies.
It was like eating between rows of morris dancers –
Only they didn't kick.

On my left sat the prince;
On my right, his drunken aide.
The frogs' thighs leapt into the sad purple face
Like fish to the sound of a Chinese flute.
I wanted to talk to the prince. I wish now
I had collared his aide, who was Saloth Sar's brother.
We treated him as the club bore. He was always
Boasting of his connections, boasting with a head-shake
Or by pronouncing of some doubtful phrase.
And well might he boast. Saloth Sar, for instance,
Was Pol Pot's real name. The APCs
Fired into the sugar palms but met no resistance.

In a diary, I refer to Pol Pot's brother as the Jockey Cap.
A few weeks later, I find him 'in good form
And very skeptical about Chantaraingsey.'
'But one eats well there,' I remark.
'So one should,' says the Jockey Cap:
'The tiger always eats well,
It eats the raw flesh of the deer,
And Chantaraingsey was born in the year of the tiger.
So, did they show you the things they do
With the young refugee girls?'

And he tells me how he will one day give me the gen.
He will tell me how the prince financed the casino
And how the casino brought Lon Nol to power.
He will tell me this.
He will tell me all these things.
All I must do is drink and listen.

In those days, I thought that when the game was up
The prince would be far, far away –
In a limestone faubourg, on the promenade at Nice,
Reduced in circumstances but well enough provided for.
In Paris, he would hardly require his private army.
The Jockey Cap might suffice for café warfare,
And matchboxes for APCs.

But we were always wrong in these predictions.
It was a family war. Whatever happened,
The principals were obliged to attend its issue.
A few were cajoled into leaving, a few were expelled,
And there were villains enough, but none of them
Slipped away with the swag.

For the prince was fighting Sihanouk, his nephew,
And the Jockey Cap was ranged against his brother
Of whom I remember nothing more
Than an obscure reputation for virtue.
I have been told that the prince is still fighting
Somewhere in the Cardamoms or the Elephant Mountains.
But I doubt that the Jockey Cap would have survived his good
                                                    connections.

I think the lunches would have done for him –
Either the lunches or the dead soldiers.

Lines for Translation into Any Language

1. I saw that the shanty town had grown over the graves and that the crowd lived among the memorials.

2. It was never very cold – a parachute slung between an angel and an urn afforded shelter for the newcomers.

3. Wooden beds were essential.

4. These people kept their supplies of gasoline in litre bottles, which their children sold at the cemetery gates.

5. That night the city was attacked with rockets.

6. The firebrigade bided its time.

7. The people dug for money beneath their beds, to pay the firemen.

8. The shanty town was destroyed, the cemetery restored.

9. Seeing a plane shot down, not far from the airport, many of the foreign community took fright.

10. The next day, they joined the queues at the gymnasium, asking to leave.

11. When the victorious army arrived, they were welcomed by the firebrigade.

12. This was the only spontaneous demonstration in their favour.

13. Other spontaneous demonstrations in their favour were organised by the victors.

Children in Exile
To J, T, L & S

'What I am is not important, whether I live or die –
   It is the same for me, the same for you.
What we do is important. This is what I have learnt.
   It is not what we are but what we do,'

Says a child in exile, one of a family
   Once happy in its size. Now there are four
Students of calamity, graduates of famine,
   Those whom geography condemns to war,

Who have settled here perforce in a strange country,
   Who are not even certain where they are.
They have learnt much. There is much more to learn.
   Each heart bears a diploma like a scar –

A red seal, always hot, always solid,
   Stamped with the figure of an overseer,
A lethal boy who has learnt to despatch with a mattock,
   Who rules a village with sharp leaves and fear.

From five years of punishment for an offence
   It took America five years to commit
These victim-children have been released on parole.
   They will remember all of it.

They have found out : it is hard to escape from Cambodia,
   Hard to escape the justice of Pol Pot,
When they are called to report in dreams to their tormentors.
   One night is merciful, the next is not.

I hear a child moan in the next room and I see
　The nightmare spread like rain across his face
And his limbs twitch in some vestigial combat
　In some remembered place.

Oh let us not be condemned for what we are.
　It is enough to account for what we do.
Save us from the judge who says : You are your father's son,
　One of your father's crimes – your crime is you.

And save us too from that fatal geography
　Where vengeance is impossible to halt.
And save Cambodia from threatened extinction.
　Let not its history be made its fault.

They feared these woods, feared tigers, snakes and malaria.
　They thought the landscape terrible and wild.
There were ghosts under the beds in the tower room.
　A hooting owl foretold a still-born child.

And how would they survive the snows of Italy?
　For the first weeks, impervious to relief,
They huddled in dark rooms and feared the open air,
　Caught in the tight security of grief.

Fear attacked the skin and made the feet swell
　Though they were bathed in tamarind at night.
Fear would descend like a swarm of flying ants.
　It was impossible to fight.

I saw him once, doubled in pain, scratching his legs.
　This was in Pisa at the Leaning Tower.
We climbed to the next floor and his attackers vanished
　As fast as they had come. He thought some power,

Some influence lurked in certain rooms and corners.
   But why was I not suffering as well?
He trod cautiously over the dead in the Campo Santo
   And saw the fading punishments of Hell

And asked whether it is true that the unjust will be tormented
   And whether those who suffer will be saved.
There are so many martyrdoms in the beautiful galleries.
   He was a connoisseur among the graves.

It was the first warm day of the year. The university
   Gossipped in friendly groups around the square.
He envied the students their marvellous education,
   Greedy for school, frantic to be in there.

On the second train he was relaxed and excited.
   For the first time he was returning home,
Pointing his pocket camera at the bright infinity of mountains.
   The winter vines shimmered like chromosomes,

Meaningless to him. The vines grew. The sap returned.
   The land became familiar and green.
The brave bird-life of Italy began planning families.
   It was the season of the selfish gene.

Lovers in cars defied the mad gynaecologist.
   In shady lanes, and later than they should,
They were watching the fireflies' brilliant use of the hyphen
   And the long dash in the darkening wood.

And then they seemed to check the car's suspension
   Or test the maximum back-axle load.
I love this valley, but I often wonder why
   There's always one bend extra in the road.

And what do the dogs defend behind the high wire fences?
  What home needs fury on a running lead?
Why did the Prince require those yellow walls?
  These private landscapes must be wealth indeed.

But you, I am glad to say, are not so fortified.
  The land just peters out behind the house.
(Although, the first time the hunters came blazing through the garden,
  Someone screamed at me : 'Get out there. What are you, man or
                                                        mouse?')

When Duschko went mad and ate all those chickens
  It was a cry for help. Now he breaks loose
And visits his fellow guards, and laughs at their misery –
  Unhappy dog ! So sensitive to abuse.

He thought there was a quantum of love and attention
  Which now he would be forced to share around
As first three Vietnamese and then four Cambodians
  Trespassed on his ground.

It doesn't work like that. It never has done.
  Love is accommodating. It makes space.
When they were requested to abandon their home in the hayloft,
  Even the doves retired with better grace.

They had the tower still, with its commanding eyelets.
  The tiles were fond of them, the sky grew kind.
They watched a new provider spreading corn on the zinc tray
  And didn't mind.

Boat people, foot people, wonky Yankee publishers –
  They'd seen the lot. They knew who slept in which beds.
They swooped down to breakfast after a night on the tiles
  And dropped a benediction on your heads.

33

And now the school bus comes honking through the valley
   And education litters every room —
Grammars, vocabularies, the Khao-i-Dang hedge dictionary,
   The future perfect, subjunctive moods and gloom.

So many questions in urgent need of answer :
   What is a Pope? What is a proper noun?
Where is Milan? Who won the Second World War?
   How many fluid ounces in a pound?

La Normandie est renommée par ses falaises et ses fromages.
   What are Normandy, cliffs, cheeses and fame?
Too many words on the look-out for too many meanings.
   Too many syllables for the tongue to frame.

A tiny philosopher climbs onto my knee
   And sinks his loving teeth into my arm.
He has had a good dream. A friendly gun-toting Jesus
   Has spent the night protecting him from harm.

He goes for Technical Lego and significant distinctions.
   Suppose, he says, I have a house and car,
Money and everything, I could lose it all,
   As we lost all our property in the war.

But if I have knowledge, if I know five languages,
   If I have mathematics and the rest,
No one can steal that from me. The difference is :
   No one inherits what I once possessed.

When I die, my education dies with me.
   I cannot leave my knowledge to my son,
Says this boy in exile, and he shrugs and laughs shortly.
   Whoever dreamt of Jesus with a gun?

His brother dreams all night of broken chords
   And all the summer long his broken hand,
Still callosed from hard labour, figures out a prelude.
   Music and maths are what he understands.

These dreams are messages. One of the dead sisters
   Says to the girl : 'Do not be sad for me.
I am alive and in your twin sister's womb
   In California, as you shall see.'

Some time later, the postman brings a letter from America.
   The child bride is expecting her first child.
Months afterwards, a photograph of a little girl.
   Something is reconciled.

Alone in the tower room, the twin keeps up her dancing.
   For the millionth time, Beethoven's *Für Elise!*
Little Vietnam borrows little Cambodia's toys.
   Mother America is the appeaser.

Pretending to work, I retire to the study
   And find a copy of *The Dyer's Hand*
Where I read : 'An emigrant never knows what he wants,
   Only what he does not want.' I understand

What it is I have seen, how simple and how powerful
   This flight, this negative ambition is
And how a girl in exile can gaze down into an olive grove
   And wonder : 'Is America like this ?'

For it is we, not they, who cannot forgive America,
   And it is we who travel, they who flee,
We who may choose exile, they who are forced out,
   Take to the hot roads, take to the sea,

In dangerous camps between facing armies,
    The prey of pirates, raped, plundered or drowned,
In treacherous waters, in single file through the minefields,
    Praying to stave off death till they are found,

Begging for sponsors, begging for a Third Country,
    Begging America to take them in –
It is they, it is they who put everything in hazard.
    What we do decides whether they sink or swim.

Do they know what they want? They know what they do not want.
    Better the owl before dawn than the devil by day.
Better strange food than famine, hard speech than mad labour.
    Better this quietness than that dismay.

Better ghosts under the bed than to sleep in the paddy.
    Better this frost, this blizzard than that sky.
Better a concert pianist than a corpse, an engineer than a shadow.
    Better to dance under the fresco than to die.

Better a new god with bleeding hands and feet,
    Better the painted tortures of the blest
Than the sharp leaf at the throat, the raised mattock
    And all the rest.

My dear American friends, I can't say how much it means to me
    To see this little family unfurl,
To see them relax and learn, and learn about happiness,
    The mother growing strong, the boys adept, the girl

Confident in your care. They can never forget the past.
    Let them remember, but let them not fear.
Let them find their future is delightfully accomplished
    And find perhaps America is here.

Let them come to the crest of the road when the morning is fine
   With Florence spread like honey on the plain,
Let them walk through the ghostless woods, let the guns be silent,
   The tiger never catch their eye again.

They are thriving I see. I hope they always thrive
   Whether in Italy, England or France.
Let them dream as they wish to dream. Let them dream

Of Jesus, America, maths, Lego, music and dance.

III

Wind

This is the wind, the wind in a field of corn.
Great crowds are fleeing from a major disaster
Down the long valleys, the green swaying wadis,
Down through the beautiful catastrophe of wind.

Families, tribes, nations and their livestock
Have heard something, seen something. An expectation
Or a gigantic misunderstanding has swept over the hilltop
Bending the ear of the hedgerow with stories of fire and sword.

I saw a thousand years pass in two seconds.
Land was lost, languages rose and divided.
This lord went east and found safety.
His brother sought Africa and a dish of aloes.

Centuries, minutes later, one might ask
How the hilt of a sword wandered so far from the smithy.
And somewhere they will sing : 'Like chaff we were borne
In the wind.' This is the wind in a field of corn.

Prison Island

That's the Naples packet slipping out of the harbour
With a fat Bourbon guard and a hold full of capers
So perhaps my letter will have escaped the censors.
But I have no news. What change could there possibly be?
Except that the rats have got at the Indian figs,

Water is low again and the trip I was planning
Across the jagged headland to explore the next cove
Has been forbidden. How are we supposed to survive
On these dry terraces, under a haze but no cloud?
Summer has even deprived us of our wider view.

We think we are in a great ocean miles from our homes.
Then one morning, waking after a trivial storm,
We find the curtains lifted and the panorama
Temptingly displayed once more. The sea becomes a lake
Whose farthest shore is Sicily where the native towns

Of my defeated friends pursue their normal business.
Beneath the coast a sail suddenly catches the wind
And becomes visible – a tan sail on a grey ship.
I wish that I had never heard these people's music
Which burdens the mind with the gloom of false memory

Making me dream recently of going home to you.
The city gate was locked but I walked through noiselessly
Along the colonnades. It was dark. Shutters contained
All that was left of conversation in the houses.
The bright conspirators were dead with their feeble jokes

And sat still at the tables of the artists' café
In their old attitudes, one with his arms stretched outwards
Encompassing a point that was lethally untrue.
There in the doorway, caught tossing his cloak for effect,
Stood the bringer of bad news whom none of us believed.

I walked on, hoping perhaps to find you still awake,
And turning by the town hall came into a new square.
Wooden scaffolding still enclosed the triumphal arch
But the vast galleries were open to the moonlight
And the smug granite facings were gleamingly polished.

An equestrian statue provided the focus –
Though not for the nightwatchmen playing cards by its plinth.
Summoning my courage I approached them to enquire
In whose honour all these renovations had been made.
The guards ignored me. I realised I too was dead.

My dear friend, do you value the counsels of dead men?
I should say this. Fear defeat. Keep it before your mind
As much as victory. Defeat at the hands of friends,
Defeat in the plans of your confident generals.
Fear the kerchiefed captain who does not think he can die.

New prisoners bring news. The evening air unravels
The friendly scents from fruit-trees, creepers and trellised vines.
In airless rooms, conversations are gently renewed.
An optimist licking his finger detects a breeze
And I begin to ignore the insidious voice

Which insists in whispers : The chance once lost is life lost
For the idea, for the losers and for their dead
Whose memorials will never be honoured or built
Until they and those they have betrayed are forgotten –
Not this year, not next year, not in your time.

Nest of Vampires

From the bare planks the reflected sun lights up
The white squares on the wall released by pictures
Depicting Tivoli, an imperial
   Family in its humiliation,
     Cows up to their knees in a cool stream

And a man in Dovedale reaching for a branch.
What fell behind the desk, what levelled the leg
Of the card-table, what had been presumed lost
   Has been found. In that chest there was a box
     Containing a piece of white coral,

A silver cigar-cutter shaped like a pike,
A chipping taken from the Great Pyramid
And a tribal fetish stolen during war :
   'This is something shameful. You must never
     Mention its existence to a soul.'

But there was so much one should never mention.
If one day those three turbaned Sikhs were announced
To have taken lodgings down in the village
   Or if, walking at evening through the grounds,
     Where the wild garlic and the old fence

Announced our boundary, my dog had halted,
Its skin bristling as it whimpered at nothing,
I should hardly have been very much surprised.
   Who goes there? Only the chalk-faced old man
     Who traps the birds under the fruit-nets

And carries them off inside his stovepipe hat.
And here in dreams comes the doll, Attic Margot,
Who drowned in the watergarden during Lent.
    She's kept her stuffing well over the years
      But the china face has quite collapsed.

'Stop talking about money. You've upset the child.'
But it wasn't that that made me cry. 'Only
A German song we have been learning at school,
    A song about the rooks building their nests
      In the high trees.' The garden is dark

But still the evil crimson of the roses
Shines through. 'I wasn't listening. Suppose
We do suddenly have to leave this old house –
    Why should that worry you? I hate it all,
      And all the children here hate me too.'

I used to think that just by counting windows
And finding secret rooms, I would come across
A clue. One evening I waited in the park
    Expecting a figure with an oil lamp
      To come to the casement and signal.

Now I stroll further afield, beyond the lodge,
And wonder why the villages are empty
And how my father lost all his money.
    I keep meeting a demented beggar
      Who mutters about the mouldiwarps

With tears in his eyes. The house is all packed up
Except for one mirror which could not be moved.
In its reflection the brilliant lawns stretch down.
'Where's that wretched boy?' I'm going now
And soon I am going to find out.

A Vacant Possession

In a short time we shall have cleared the gazebo.
Look how you can scrape the weeds from the paving stones
With a single motion of the foot. Paths lead down
Past formal lawns, orchards, notional guinea-fowl
To where the house is entirely obscured from view.

And there are gravel drives beneath the elm-tree walks
On whose aquarium green the changing weather
Casts no shadow. Urns pour their flowers out beside
A weathered Atlas with the whole world to support.
Look, it is now night and there are lights in the trees.

The difficult guest is questioning his rival.
He is pacing up and down while she leans against
A mossy water-butt in which, could we see them,
Innumerable forms of life are uncurving.
She is bravely not being hurt by his manner

Of which they have warned her. He taps his cigarette
And brusquely changed the subject. He remembers
Something said earlier which she did not really mean.
Nonsense – she did mean it. Now he is satisfied.
She has bitten the quick of her thumb-nail, which bleeds.

What shall we do the next day? The valley alters.
You set out from the village and the road turns around,
So that, in an hour, behind a clump of oak-trees,
With a long whitewashed wall and a low red-tiled roof
Peaceful, unevenly they appear again.

The square, the café seats, the doorways are empty
And the long grey balconies stretch out on all sides.
Time for an interlude, evening in the country,
With distant cowbells providing the angelus.
But we are interrupted by the latest post.

'Of course you will never understand. How could you?
You had everything. Everything always went well
For you. If there was a court at which I could sue you
I should take you for every memory you have.
No doubt you are insured against your murdered friends.'

Or : 'We see very little of Hester these days.
Why don't you come home? Your room is as you left it.
I went in yesterday, looking for notepaper,
And – do you know – the noose is still over the bed!
Archie says he will bring it out to you this summer.'

On warm spring afternoons, seated in the orchard,
The smocked, serious students develop grave doubts
About Pascal's wager. Monsieur le Curé stays
Chatting till midnight over the porcelain stove.
The last of his nine proofs lies smouldering in the grate.

I have set up my desk in an old dressing-room
So that the shadow of the fig-tree will be cast
On this page. At night, on the mountain opposite,
The beam of approaching cars is seen in the sky.
And now a slamming door and voices in the hall,

Scraping suitcases and laughter. Shall I go down?
I hear my name called, peer over the bannister
And remember something I left in my bedroom.
What can it have been? The window is wide open.
The curtains move. The light sways. The cold sets in.

Vuccerìa

Maybe this summer I shall revisit Palermo
And see if the Shanghai restaurant is still there
And if you can still buy cartons of contraband
Cigarettes in the triangular square
Beneath. At evening the horses are undressed
From top to toe, in the nude light-bulbs' glare.
They leave their skeletons ever so neatly folded
And piled. Look ! there's a pair of socks,
Crimson with two black clocks.
              Oh no it isn't.
It's a flayed head on a bedside chair.

Chosun

So the Chosunese would imagine the earth to be flat,
'Hooked onto eternity in some way by the corners,'
And they marked their charts : volcanoes, no leisure,
One-eyed, great joy, long deserts, converging curves,

There were large people, white people, overflowing people, reciprocal
    people,
Immortal, cross-legged, perforated, hoary,
Among beautiful clouds, summer prefecture, breathing peace,
    perennial hemp,
There were sorcerers, deep-eyed, mulberry and pear, without entrails.

Then there were chest-binders, fire-rejecters, rice-eaters, hat-band-
    holders,
Clear-footed, three-bodied, fork-tongued, rat-named,
With helmet-wearers, ear-nippers and those who spin silk from the
    mouth,
There were women, virtuous women and the chief astronomers of Yoo,

Who drank boiled iris root against feeblemindedness.
A wonderful cure for headaches was made
From dog's testicle flower. Honeysuckle
Was a poultice for boils. Forget Your Troubles

Was a poison. Jewelweed also, for a violent purge
After spoiled meat, or garlic for an antidote
Which reduced hypertension, or tigerlily for a cough.
Morning Glory was the symbol of a superficial man.

They made the coastline terrible to strangers
And in the interior whole forests were burned down
And the mountains were kept bare until the topsoil
Washed clean away, to discourage tigers.

But there were leopards and wolves in the unfashionable quarters
Of town, and hordes of masterless dogs
And scavenging pigs among the canals and sewers.
There was smallpox, cholera, typhoid and polio.

The traitors' heads were exposed on the tower gates.
Squads of soldiers with single-shot rifles
Moved through the city. For their greater safety
They carried no ammunition. Bayonets were fixed.

At sunset the fires in the hills announced
That Chosun was at peace. The men retired indoors
And the women were allowed onto the streets for one hour.
Then woe betide any man who ventured forth.

The women were summoned home with gongs at curfew.
They measured their husbands' love according the strictness of their
    isolation.
The husbands were attracted by the upward curve of the big toe.
Love did not make a marriage. Love grew later.

Night belonged to the women and to their work
And their shrill gossip which carried through the darkness.
The men slept or went to court. By ancient custom
All the palace woke at night, for safety's sake.

One lived in Seoul, or one lived in disgrace
In an obscure retreat which it was impolite to disturb.
Pyongyang lay to the north. It was known
As one of the four wickedest cities of ancient or modern times.

There were no temples or places of worship in Seoul.
There were no wells in Pyongyang. The city was shaped
Like a boat. To dig for water would undoubtedly
Cause the whole boat to sink. Therefore to dig wells was treason.

The king's new alphabet made a clear distinction
Between surd and sonant. It was good for any practical use
And even the sound of the wind, the chirping of birds
And the barking of dogs could be exactly described by it.

But the scholars objected : It was a violation of faith
To invent and use letters which did not exist in China.
It was replied : If a man is accused of a capital crime
The alphabet will help him make a correct statement

And avoid prosecution. But the scholars objected :
It is not the fitness of the letters for expressing thought,
But the fairness or unfairness of the judge which decides.
So the king told a white lie : the new alphabet, he said, is Chinese.

This was the code : between friends, trust ;
Between elder and younger, respect ; between husband and wife,
Distinction in position ; between father and son,
Intimacy ; between the king and ministers, loyalty.

Somewhere there existed one God. He was kindly
But remote, and therefore of restricted interest.
The women worshipped the devils which swarmed
Like disease – or they pretended to worship them,

For although the devils' power for evil was unlimited,
Their ability to read a man's thoughts went no further
Than average human. What the devils wanted was worship.
One might pretend to worship, and thus placate them.

At every great tree in a village, at every mountain pass,
Sacrifice must be made with some part of oneself.
It was enough to spit, or leave a rag from one's clothes,
Or, for blood, a handful of sprinkled chicken's feathers.

God knew men's hearts and minds.
He would forgive the feathers, and ignore the spitting.
But the men grew impatient with the placation of devils.
Science was more dignified. So they turned

To the soft almanacs of the diviner or fortune-teller
To learn where best to select a grave-site
Through which succeeding generations would be prosperous.
It was vital to die at home, or the spirit would be restless

And it was vital to know and worship one's ancestors.
If a man's house caught fire,
It was vital to rescue the family tree.
To lose one's ancestors was permanent disgrace.

No wonder they feared war and hated foreigners,
Who marked their charts with Deception Bay,
False River and Insult Island.
Christians were especially forbidden to enter Chosun

But were not to be stopped. Disguised as mourners,
'Under a vow of silence,' their foreign faces veiled,
They passed through the Hermit Kingdom, the Land of Morning
    Calm,
Until the dogs smelled them out, and howled for their martyrdom.

The Skip

I took my life and threw it on the skip,
Reckoning the next-door neighbours wouldn't mind
If my life hitched a lift to the council tip
With their dry rot and rubble. What you find

With skips is – the whole community joins in.
Old mattresses appear, doors kind of drift
Along with all that won't fit in the bin
And what the bin-men can't be fished to shift.

I threw away my life, and there it lay
And grew quite sodden. 'What a dreadful shame,'
Clucked some old bag and sucked her teeth : 'The way
The young these days . . . no values . . . me, I blame . . .'

But I blamed no one. Quality control
Had loused it up, and that was that. 'Nough said.
I couldn't stick at home. I took a stroll
And passed the skip, and left my life for dead.

Without my life, the beer was just as foul,
The landlord still as filthy as his wife,
The chicken in the basket was an owl,
And no one said : 'Ee, Jim-lad, whur's thee life?'

Well, I got back that night the worse for wear,
But still just capable of single vision ;
Looked in the skip ; my life – it wasn't there !
Some bugger'd nicked it – *without* my permission.

Okay, so I got angry and began
To shout, and woke the street. Okay. *Okay!*
And I was sick all down the neighbour's van.
And I disgraced myself on the par-*kay.*

And then . . . you know how if you've had a few
You'll wake at dawn, all healthy, like sea breezes,
Raring to go, and thinking : 'Clever you !
You've got away with it.' And then, oh Jesus,

It hits you. Well, that morning, just at six
I woke, got up and looked down at the skip.
There lay my life, still sodden, on the bricks ;
There lay my poor old life, arse over tip.

Or was it mine? Still dressed, I went downstairs
And took a long cool look. The truth was dawning.
Someone had just exchanged my life for theirs.
Poor fool, I thought – I should have left a warning.

Some bastard saw my life and thought it nicer
Than what he had. Yet what he'd had seemed fine.
He'd never caught his fingers in the slicer
The way I'd managed in that life of mine.

His life lay glistening in the rain, neglected,
Yet still a decent, an authentic life.
Some people I can think of, I reflected
Would take that thing as soon as you'd say Knife.

It seemed a shame to miss a chance like that.
I brought the life in, dried it by the stove.
It looked so fetching, stretched out on the mat.
I tried it on. It fitted, like a glove.

56

And now, when some local bat drops off the twig
And new folk take the house, and pull up floors
And knock down walls and hire some kind of big
Container (say, a skip) for their old doors,

I'll watch it like a hawk, and every day
I'll make at least – oh – half a dozen trips.
I've furnished an existence in that way.
You'd not believe the things you find on skips.

A Staffordshire Murderer

Every fear is a desire. Every desire is fear.
The cigarettes are burning under the trees
Where the Staffordshire murderers wait for their accomplices
And victims. Every victim is an accomplice.

It takes a lifetime to stroll to the carpark
Stopping at the footbridge for reassurance,
Looking down at the stream, observing
(With one eye) the mallard's diagonal progress backwards.

You could cut and run, now. It is not too late.
But your fear is like a long-case clock
In the last whirring second before the hour,
The hammer drawn back, the heart ready to chime.

Fear turns the ignition. The van is unlocked.
You may learn now what you ought to know :
That every journey begins with a death,
That the suicide travels alone, that the murderer needs company.

And the Staffordshire murderers, nervous though they are,
Are masters of the conciliatory smile.
A cigarette? A tablet in a tin?
Would you care for a boiled sweet from the famous poisoner

Of Rugeley? These are his own brand.
He has never had any complaints.
He speaks of his victims as a sexual braggart
With a tradesman's emphasis on the word 'satisfaction'.

You are flattered as never before. He appreciates
So much, the little things – your willingness for instance
To bequeath your body at once to his experiments.
He sees the point of you as no one else does.

Large parts of Staffordshire have been undermined.
The trees are in it up to their necks. Fish
Nest in their branches. In one of the Five Towns
An ornamental pond disappeared overnight

Dragging the ducks down with it, down to the old seams
With a sound as of a gigantic bath running out,
Which is in turn the sound of ducks in distress.
Thus History murders mallards, while we hear nothing

Or what we hear we do not understand.
It is heard as the tramp's rage in the crowded precinct :
'Woe to the bloody city of Lichfield.'
It is lost in the enthusiasm of the windows

From which we are offered on the easiest terms
Five times over in colour and once in monochrome
The first reprisals after the drill-sergeant's coup.
How speedily the murder detail makes its way

Along the green beach, past the pink breakers,
And binds the whole cabinet to the oil-drums,
Where death is a preoccupied tossing of the head,
Where no decorative cloud lingers at the gun's mouth.

At the Dame's School dust gathers on the highwayman,
On Sankey and Moody, Wesley and Fox,
On the snoring churchwarden, on Palmer the Poisoner
And Palmer's house and Stanfield Hall.

The brilliant moss has been chipped from the Red Barn.
They say that Cromwell played ping-pong with the cathedral.
We train roses over the arches. In the Minster Pool
Crayfish live under carved stones. Every spring

The rats pick off the young mallards and
The good weather brings out the murderers
By the Floral Clock, by the footbridge,
The pottery murderers in jackets of prussian blue.

'Alack, George, where are thy shoes?'
He lifted up his head and espied the three
Steeple-house spires, and they struck at his life.
And he went by his eye over hedge and ditch

And no one laid hands on him, and he went
Thus crying through the streets, where there seemed
To be a channel of blood running through the streets,
And the market-place appeared like a pool of blood.

For this field of corpses was Lichfield
Where a thousand Christian Britons fell
In Diocletian's day, and 'much could I write
Of the sense that I had of the blood –'

That winter Friday. Today it is hot.
The cowparsley is so high that the van cannot be seen
From the road. The bubbles rise in the warm canal.
Below the lock-gates you can hear mallards.

A coot hurries along the tow-path, like a Queen's Messenger.
On the heli-pad, an arrival in blue livery
Sends the water-boatmen off on urgent business.
News of a defeat. Keep calm. The cathedral chimes.

The house by the bridge is the house in your dream.
It stares through new frames, unwonted spectacles,
And the paint, you can tell, has been weeping.
In the yard, five striped oildrums. Flowers in a tyre.

This is where the murderer works. But it is Sunday.
Tomorrow's bank holiday will allow the bricks to set.
You see? he has thought of everything. He shows you
The snug little cavity he calls 'your future home'.

And 'Do you know,' he remarks, 'I have been counting my victims.
Nine hundred and ninety nine, the Number of the Beast!
That makes you . . .' But he sees he has overstepped the mark :
'I'm sorry, but you cannot seriously have thought you were the first?'

A thousand preachers, a thousand poisoners,
A thousand martyrs, a thousand murderers –
Surely these preachers are poisoners, these martyrs murderers?
Surely this is all a gigantic mistake?

But there has been no mistake. God and the weather are glorious.
You have come as an anchorite to kneel at your funeral.
Kneel then and pray. The blade flashes a smile.
This is your new life. This murder is yours.

IV

Letter
to
John Fuller
(1972)

Je tire ainsi de l'absurde trois conséquences qui sont ma révolte, ma liberté et ma passion. Par le seul jeu de la conscience, je transforme en règle de vie ce qui était invitation à la mort – et je refuse le suicide . . . Maintenant, il s'agit de vivre.

Camus, *Le Mythe de Sisyphe*

Letter to John Fuller

Poets, from paupers to well-heeled,
The best the British side can field,
Whose paradise the muse revealed,
   Out of your narcol –
eptic repose rise up to wield
   Your desperate charcoal.

Practitioners of Ethnic Verse,
Garrulous Scots and Welshmen terse
And Fenian bibbers of the Erse
   Castalian fountain,
You ardent fans of St.-John Perse
   And the Black Mountain.

Dull imagists, the strictly free,
Po-faced admirers of H.D.
The reticent, like Laurie Lee,
   Sci-Fi Tellurians,
Blood-and-guts men, the limply twee
   And you, Arthurians,

Old soaks from former poets' pubs
And after-hours drinking clubs,
Rouged admen, rugose Fleet Street subs,
   Exiles from the Bronx,
People with names like Frederick Grubb's
   Or Rosemary Tonks',

From cottages weighed down with blooms,
From frozen tarns, from windswept cwms,
From Rachman-run bedsitting-rooms
  In Potters Bar,
Emerge like mummies from your tombs
  And show some *ka*.

Release that shuttle, drop that bottle,
Leave on the settle Kettle, Pottle,
For someone's come I bet'll throttle
  Your idiot soirées –
A man of mettle every sot'll
  Worship – ALVAREZ!

Alvarez – och the clap o' thundy,
Like some great shape from *Spiritus Mundi*,
A seven days' man like Solomon Grundy,
  Or *7 Days*,
Oh spread the news from Eigg to Lundy
  For Al's the craze.

Alfresco, Al Capone, Alaskan,
Alhambra, *alla marcia*, ask an
Average, well-read Nebraskan –
  He'll know the style.
He'd recognise Al with a mask on
  At half a mile.

Al Jolson, allotrope, Aleutian,
Alembic, allophone, don't you shun
The subject, if you're in confusion –
  West of the Drina
He's just as modish as pollution,
  Though slightly cleaner.

Is your muse flat? He'll reinflate her.
Hungry? He steps up like a waiter.
Are you a fan of Walter Pater?
   He'll only scoff.
His measurements would shame a satyr
   When he peels off.

He knows what makes the poet tick.
   He knows society is sick.
Gentility just gets his wick –
   It makes him scowl
With rage. His hide is tough and thick
   As a boiled owl.

He tells you, in the sombrest notes,
If poets want to get their oats
The first step is to slit their throats.
   The way to divide
The sheep of poetry from the goats
   Is suicide.

Hardy and Hopkins hacked off their honkers.
Auden took laudanum in Yonkers.
Yeats ate a fatal plate of conkers.
   On Margate sands
Eliot was found stark staring bonkers
   Slashing his hands.

'Jug-jug-jug-jugular,' he cried,
Then leapt into the sea and died.
His corpse returned on the next tide.
   They built a pyre.
All through his wretched life, they sighed,
   He had lacked fire.

You know how Wallace Stevens went?
He bit the bullet in Stoke-on-Trent.
Ere half her speckled span was spent
    Marianne Moore
Donned her best hat, then out she leant
    From the tenth floor.

What Yevtushenko lacked in vim
He made up with a long and grim
Self-immolation. On a whim
    Pablo Neruda
Took with him when he went to swim
    A barracuda.

Examples of this sort abound.
The rest I'll leave Al to expound.
There's so much suicide around
    I'm frankly staggered
That any work gets off the ground
    Before we're knackered.

For a poet, not to have cut his wrist
Is worse than having not been kissed.
And surely, *si vous suivez ma piste*,
    It's somewhat eerie
That so few novelists insist
    On *hara kiri*

Or an elaborate *seppuku*.
Which brings me to my purpose. Look you,
John Fuller, I admire your book. You
    Write well, though sanely.
You're also an exquisite cook. (You
    Do Chinese, mainly.)

Your style's complex and problematical.
Rarely do you appear fanatical.
Your dominant humour is phlegmatical.
   What could be more highly ag-
reeable than four months sabbatical
   In Gallt-y-Ceiliog.

But frankly this is not enough.
Great poets come from sterner stuff.
Their voices should be deep and gruff,
   Urgent and things,
Not like the tones of Master Lough
   Singing 'Oh for the Wings'.

This is of course the Brownjohn view –
And I'm as much to blame as you.
For a poet to heave into view –
   To be *emergent* –
He must whine, as if he wants the loo,
   'Please sir, I'm *urgent*.'

Now *urgency* is just Al's thing,
His stock-in-trade, as 'twere his *Ding
An sich*. Never since Wagner's *Ring*,
   Or perhaps Gluck,
Has *urgency* had such a fling
   As in his book.

I'm feeling *urgent* as I write.
Three times I've woken in the night.
Twice, when my pen was in full flight,
   I've had to dash
Bursting with inner rage and spite
   And want of cash.

I've just decided what to do.
For months now I've been dreadfully blue
Since first I had the chance to view
   Al's handsome head
Pictured on the *Observer Review*
   Lying as dead.

Look John, I trust your sense of tact.
Why don't you join me in the act?
Perhaps we could devise a pact,
   A Grand Last Bow.
For omelettes, eggs must first be cracked.
   Let's crack ours, now.

Should we take hemlock? Too abstruse.
A punch of deadly nightshade juice?
A dressing-gown cord for a noose?
   Strychnine-soaked spats?
Alas! Warfarin is no more use
   For poets or rats.

Let's make our suicide really gay.
It is the most aggressive way
Of being superior. You say
   Your life is inner.
So is the man's who cannot pay
   For the next dinner.

Let's order a banquet just for us.
Let's wail and moan and make a fuss,
Then throw ourselves beneath a bus –
   Show them we're serious
And we don't give a tinker's cuss.
   Let's be mysterious.

Death is the envy of the hicks,
The last crap shot, the final fix,
It is the burning of the ricks.
    Lovelier than sex, it
Beckons us home across the Styx
    And we must exit.

V

Exempla
(1968-1970)

The general design of the following sheets is to inlist Imagination under the banner of Science ; and to lead her votaries from the looser analogies, which dress out the imagery of poetry, to the stricter ones which form the ratiocination of philosophy.

Poetry admits of very few words expressive of perfectly abstracted ideas, whereas Prose abounds with them. And as our ideas derived from visible objects are more distinct than those of our other senses, the words expressive of these ideas belonging to vision make up the principle part of poetic language. That is the Poet writes principally to the eye.

The matter must be interesting from its sublimity, beauty, or novelty : this is the scientific part ; and the art consists in bringing these distinctly before the eye.

Erasmus Darwin

Exempla

A frog hunts on land by vision. He escapes
Enemies mainly by seeing them. His eyes
Do not move, as do ours, to follow prey,
Attend suspicious events, or search
For things of interest. If his body changes
Its position with respect to gravity or the whole
Visual world is rotated around him,
Then he shows compensatory eye-movements. These

Movements enter his hunting and evading
Habits only, e.g. as he sits
On a rocking lily pad. Thus his eyes
Are actively stabilised. The frog does not seem
To see, or at any rate is not concerned with
The detail of the stationary world around him.
He will starve to death surrounded by food
If it is not moving. His choice of food

Is determined only by size and movement.
He will leap to capture any object the size
Of an insect or worm provided it moves
Like one. He can be fooled easily not only
By a piece of dangled meat but by any
Small moving object. His sex life
Is conducted by sound and touch. His choice
Of paths in escaping enemies does not

Seem to be governed by anything more devious
Than leaping to where it is darker. Since
He is equally at home on water and on land,
Why should it matter where he lights
After jumping, or what particular direction
He takes? He does remember a living
Thing provided it stays within
His field of vision and he is not distracted.

2.

Psychopharmacological drugs
which are claimed to be active in the clinic,
whether anti-depressant like imipramine,
or antipsychotic or neuroleptic
like reserpine or chlorpromazine,
have very marked anti-mescaline activity

in the mouse.

3.

For the context of the basidiocarp Singer states :
'. . . context yellow or white,
changing or unchanging,
often blue at the base of the stipe,
otherwise not blue or bluing . . .
all hyphae without clamp connections . . .'

4.

The genus Stephanoma
was established by Wallroth in 1833
on the basis of Stephanoma Strigosum,
the type of the genus. Wallroth
described the fungus as possessing
a pezizaform hairy sporochodium
with a flattened powdery surface layer
of globose, vesiculate, hyaline conidia.

5.

The obsolete Oxfordshire game of 'A-All'. Played with a large wooden die, the faces marked with the letters A, P, T, N, H, O respectively. Each player put marbles in a ring marked on the ground. The die was thrown and if

A came uppermost he took *all*
P came uppermost he *put* one in
T came uppermost he *took* one
N came uppermost he took *none*
H came uppermost he took *half*
O came uppermost he was *out*

and another took the die.

6.

GIRL ATTACKED
Police seek Tattooed Man

7.

Adult: That's a tattooed man.
Child: Tooman. Tattoo man. Find too tattoo man. Tattoo man. Who dat? Tattoo. Too man go, mommy? Too man. Tattoo man go? Who dat? Read dat. Tractor dere. Tattoo man.

8.

A voice disguiser with membrane of a spider's egg-case made from the wing-bone of a large bird. Women may not see this instrument.

9.

come and eat your Pablum

10.

Sweden. Lapp. Pouch made from a blackthroated diver (*Colymbus Articus*). Male specimen, probably taken in the nuptial season.

Eastern Eskimo. Iglulik Tribe. Pouch made from the footskin of an albatross. Collected during Admiral Sir Leopold McClintock's expedition in H.M.S. *Fox*. 1859.

Faroe Islands. Strono Kvivig. House broom of four puffin's wings.

11.

In September greasebands are put on standard apple, pear, plum and cherry trees to catch those wingless moths which must walk to their business.

It has been said that the male winter moth will take the female for a ride and fly her over the sticky barrier of tree grease. Such efforts must be casual acts of gallantry, for usually the female moth crawling up the tree remains to ornament the grease.

12.

At the foot of every steep cliff or precipice in high Alpine regions, a talus is seen of rocky fragments detached by the alternate action of frost and thaw. If these loose masses, instead of accumulating on a stationary base, happen to fall upon a glacier, they will move along with it, and, in the place of a single heap, they will form in the course of years a long stream of blocks. If a glacier be 20 miles long, and its annual progression about 500 feet, it will require about two centuries for a block thus lodged upon its surface to travel down from the higher to the lower regions, or to the extremity of the icy mass. This terminal point remains usually unchanged from year to year, although every part of the ice is in motion, because the liquefaction by heat is just sufficient to balance the onward movement of the glacier, which may be compared to an endless file of soldiers, pouring into a breach, and shot down as soon as they advance.

Lyell : *Principles of Geology*

A. The Pitt-Rivers Museum, Oxford

Is shut
22 hours a day and all day Sunday
And should not be confused
With its academic brother, full of fossils
And skeletons of bearded seals. Take
Your heart in your hand and go ; it does not sport
Any of Ruskin's hothouse Venetian
And resembles rather, with its dusty girders,
A vast gymnasium or barracks – though
The resemblance ends where

Entering
You will find yourself in a climate of nut castanets,
A musical whip
From the Torres Straits, from Mirzapur a sistrum
Called Jumka, 'used by aboriginal
Tribes to attract small game
On dark nights', a mute violin,
Whistling arrows, coolie cigarettes
And a mask of Saagga, the Devil Doctor,
The eyelids worked by strings.

Outside,
All around you, there are students researching
With a soft electronic
Hum, but here, where heels clang
On iron grates, voices are at best
Disrespectful : 'Please sir, where's the withered
Hand ?' For teachers the thesis is salutary
And simple, a hierarchy of progress culminating
In the Entrance Hall, but children are naturally
Unaware of and unimpressed by this.

Encountering
'A jay's feather worn as a charm
In Buckinghamshire, Stone',
We cannot either feel that we have come
Far or in any particular direction.
Item. A dowser's twig, used by Webb
For locating the spring, 'an excellent one',
For Lord Pembroke's waterworks at Dinton
Village. 'The violent twisting is shown
On both limbs of the fork.'

Yes
You have come upon the fabled lands where myths
Go when they die,
But some, especially the Brummagem capitalist
Juju, have arrived prematurely. Idols
Cast there and sold to tribes for a huge
Price for human sacrifice do
(Though slightly hidden) actually exist
And we do well to bring large parties
Of schoolchildren here to find them.

Outdated
Though the cultural anthropological system be
The lonely and unpopular
Might find the landscapes of their childhood marked out
Here, in the chaotic piles of souvenirs.
The claw of a condor, the jaw-bone of a dolphin,
These cleave the sky and the waves but they
Would trace from their windowseats the storm petrel's path
From Lindness or Naze to the North Cape,
Sheltered in the trough of the wave.

For the solitary,
The velveted only child who wrestled
With eagles for their feathers
And the young girl on the hill, who heard
The din on the causeway and saw the large
Hound with the strange pretercanine eyes
Herald the approach of her turbulent lover,
This boxroom of the forgotten or hardly possible
Is laid with the snares of privacy and fiction
And the dangerous third wish.

Beware.
You are entering the climate of a foreign logic
And are cursed by the hair
Of a witch, earth from the grave of a man
Killed by a tiger and a woman who died
In childbirth, 2 leaves from the tree
Azumü, which withers quickly, a nettle-leaf,
A leaf from the swiftly deciduous 'Flame of the
Forest' and a piece of a giant taro,
A strong irritant if eaten.

Go
As a historian of ideas or a sex-offender,
For the primitive art,
As a dusty semiologist, equipped to unravel
The seven components of that witch's curse
Or the syntax of the mutilated teeth. Go
In groups to giggle at curious finds.
But do not step into the kingdom of your promises
To yourself, like a child entering the forbidden
Woods of his lonely playtime :

All day,
Watching the groundsman breaking the ice
From the stone trough,
The sun slanting across the lawns, the grass
Thawing, the stable-boy blowing on his fingers,
He had known what tortures the savages had prepared
For him there, as he calmly pushed open the gate
And entered the wood near the placard : 'TAKE NOTICE
MEN-TRAPS AND SPRING-GUNS ARE SET ON THESE PREMISES.'
For his father had protected his good estate.

B. The Fruit-Grower in War-time
(and some of his enemies)

These are the problems he inherits :
Bonfire rubbish has remained unburned for months,
Dry beech leaf is accumulating under
Beech hedges, those rotten peasticks have become
Cluttered up with autumn leaves and shrubberies
    Lie thick with excellent
Weevil cover. Too late
For the administrator of Derris Dust
Since egg-laying is inside the bud. April,
He forewarned us, *is the weevil's busy month*
And the right time to employ that poison. If
    Only these weevils had been dusted

In early Spring, *the hind legs* of the
Female *are said to be* affected, thus
Cramping her style at egg-laying. Precision
Counts for much, but foresight and provision are
Mandatory if total loss is to be
    Avoided. *Egg-laying* . . .
    Before the bud-cluster
Is beyond the green-bud stage. No poison will
Affect the hatched weevil, for it when feeding
On the leaf takes only the inner tissues
And it is small comfort to the fruit-grower
    To know that it sometimes disappears

Almost as suddenly as it came.
He knows that what few apples survive attack
From weevils and mature have only to face
Further depredations from the sawfly and
Codling moth. Often, walking down orchard rows
    In summer where such pests
    Are prevalent, he has
Heard the sharp clicks as the innumerable
Apple-suckers jump from the apple leaves at
His approach, a pest whose winged generation
Can cloud the windscreens of bus-drivers in Kent.
    No wonder then that he cultivates

    Such minute accuracy. *Settling*
Herself at the edge of the calyx cup, where
Two sepals join, the sawfly faces into
The centre of the flower, bends her body down
And inserts her ovipositor into
    The side of the fruitlet.
    The eggs of the Codling
Moth are *noticeable only when the sun*
Glints on them. To control the grubs he will need
Not a single spray at petal fall (which is
Useless over a length of time) but a wash
    Between the 1st and 10th of July.

Add to this fast-growing list the two
Kinds of Capsid bug, *like a streamlined aphis*
With wings and the ability to run fast,
Which *when seen on the leaf run round to the back,*
The Woolly Aphis called American Blight,
   Which reproduces by
   Parthenogenesis,
And caterpillars of the winter moth, *both*
Those which loop and those which wriggle hastily
Backwards. The resistance is numbered but now
Little remains save twisted leaves, brown wilted
   Blossoms or dwarfed apples. Young branches

   Festooned with white felty coverings . . .
Minute punctures with reddish margins spot the
Opening leaves . . . strange little dark lines and loops . . .
The appearance of the photos of the moon . . .
Dry seas and craters . . . a nasty sour smell where
   Wet frass always exudes.
   And for the future, one
Man stands between us and worse than this, his face
Kindly, his grey hairs venerable and he
Knows what he is about. *Speak to him,* says his
Acquaintance, *at any time of the year and*
   He'll either produce from a waistcoat

Pocket a tiny glass tube with the
Choicest bugs in it, or show you ever such
A beautiful portrait of one done of course
By himself. Such diligence. We find it hard,
Knowing that a bad harvest or a poor crop
    Can overthrow a state,
    To overestimate
The value of his work. But something remains
Which gives us pause. We think of all those gallons
Of arsenate of lead being pumped over
Our native soil. How can we help comparing
    Ourselves to the last idiot heirs

Of some Roman province, still for the
Sake of form eating off lead platters? With each
Bug destroyed and apple saved we are nearer
Discovering what we are about. Meanwhile
We must observe the fruit-grower with caution
    But remember his friend's
    Stern charge that *it is you*
Who when you eat into an apple do not like to
Bite into a bug, that have led him into
His bloodthirsty way of life. One cannot doubt
That this is so and that in similar or
    Related cases the paradigm holds true.

C. South Parks Road

When they have completed its re-edification
And eradicated the tell-tale traces of its former
Yellow-bricked Gothic style, when the lease has run out for
  The Commonwealth Services Club, when the nuns
  From St Frideswide's Cherwell Edge

Gather like swallows whistling on the telegraph wires,
Why will I be bothering with my homunculus?
Already committees have been set up to decide
  On a more potent name, like Avogadro
  Avenue or Zeta Strip.

Summer has stumbled upon South Parks Road and found it
Both wilderness and formal garden, the sultry heat
Dancing the seven veils on the car-tops, blossom and
  Birdlime on windscreens and a drain spluttering
  Froth under the laburnums.

Though by the flowering cherry there is a location
For something of glamour to emerge from a lecture
Shaking its locks and swinging a satchel, while guitars
  Tell of green fields and the beau revs his MG,
  That is something I have yet

To observe. Things are unhappy. The fretful measures
Of a blackbird to secure its acid plot beneath
The Institute windows, the squirrels' precarious
  Flights down the avenue are suitable and
  Desperate appliances

At both levels. I hear a voice from a garden hut
Relating the case history of a chimpanzee
Which, faced with an elementary learning problem of
   Peanut-here or peanut-there, chose knowingly
   To administer itself

A lethal electric shock, in pique at being used
As a guinea-pig. Hunter, who was conducting the
Experiment, gives no credit to the story as
   Such. Why then, asks the voice, was the animal
   Refused Christian burial?

There is a taste associated with hot exhaust,
Of a carious tooth and nicotine on the gums
And there is a feeling as if a poisonous moth
   Had landed softly on the nape of my neck.
   The struggle is already

Over before I emerge into the street with its
Architecture of Goede Hoop. How can you expect
Me to rise to the eagle holding the rotunda
   Like a victim, if it watches the School of
   Inorganic Chemistry –

Pure Cinema Inca? I deal in minutiae,
Not with the fungus growing on the low walls but its
Globose vesiculate hyaline conidia.
   On the context of the basidiocarp
   I am seldom mistaken,

Though baffled in sunlight by gardens as fertile as
Chlorine, where the process of the seasons is something
Unfortunate. Blossom is not enough, it swirls
   In the gutters and collects at the drain-mouths.
   And besides there are stronger

Attractions at hand, the bleached facing of new buildings
And the orange cranes lit up against the cobalt sky
At evening. There is not much I could not tell about
   This road, as it is now, were the subject not
   Frustration and ignorance.

D. A Terminal Moraine

It's simple but I find it hard to explain
Why I should wish to go from the moraine.

Below me in the wide plains I can see
Straight roads through flat fields, a measured sea.

At night with its orange lamps the city raised
To a dome, the fields lost under haze.

Above where a vein of granite and a stream
Are indistinguishable sometimes the crags seem

To totter against the moving clouds. Those dots
Of orange represent climbers on the rocks.

At night I can see nothing of the valley behind,
Though from the bleating of the sheep my mind

Constructs with points as on a graph the curved
Recess. A stream gathers and swerves

A few yards before my hill. Here there are trees,
Mainly pines, and every sudden breeze

Is amplified for my benefit. I listen and in the deep
Of the night, when I am alone, I landscape my sleep.

Daylight brings company or distraction : clouds
Passing, the lichen on the rock with its loud

Disturbing yellow. Shutting my eyes
I am never alone. Each element vies,

Whether it is a birch-leaf turning in the sun
Or a car on the road. There are boys with guns

And hikers in bright socks. I do not rise early.
I eat in an orderly fashion and think clearly.

I arrange objects in rooms according to a design
And am usually presentable. If the prospect is fine

For a walk, I naturally go. There will always be
The evening for work. My decisions are free.

Except when visitors cry off or friends leave
After long weekends it is enough to deceive

The mind into employment and to give shape to thought.
And if this I could have its way it ought

To turn as a wheel in a millstream. There is peace
In this valley. Why not enjoy it? while the trees

Enchant my sleep and I become a thing
Of caves and hollows, mouths where the winds sing.

But when a car is on the road I hear
My heart beat faster as it changes gear.

VI

The Empire
of the Senseless

The Kingfisher's Boxing Gloves
(le martin-pêcheur et ses gants bourrés)
after Baudelaire

The walrus stretches forth a wrinkled hand.
The petrel winks a dull, mascaraed eye.
Dusk comes softly, treading along the sand.
Along the wet spar and the hornbeam sky
Night is secreted in the orbit's gland.
The alligator yawns and heaves a sigh.
Between its teeth, black as an upright grand,
The mastik bird performs its dentistry.

So much sand that a man at night becomes
A perfect hourglass. Out among the dunes
They stretch the vellum on the savage drums.
The hotel bar is hushed. The bootboy croons
Softly. The manager completes his sums
And shuts the register. The end of June's
The end of his season. The song he hums
Clashes at midnight with the savage tunes.

It is the marram grass, the marram grass
That soughs beneath my balcony all night,
That claws the webbed feet of the beasts that pass,
That irritates the nostrils till they fight.
Fed up with sand, tired of treading on glass,
I take the coach and leave tomorrow night
For colder, milder northern climes, alas
With friends of whom I cannot bear the sight.

The diamond cutter working for de Beers,
The lady with the yashmak from Zem-Zem,
The tattooed man, the girl with jutting ears,
The lovely bishop with the kiss-worn gem,
That pair of cataleptic engineers,
I throw out pontoon bridges to meet them
And take on new, funicular veneers,
Thanking my stars that this is just pro tem.

The cicerone is unknown to flap,
The sort of chap who never makes a slip.
He can provide the only useful map.
He tells the men how much and when to tip.
He buys the sort of rope that will not snap
On the descent. He tells you where to grip.
That it's the thirteenth step that springs the trap.
That smugglers sweat along the upper lip.

For this, much thanks. The way is often steep
And rust betrays the pitons of the blind.
The pollen count is up. The folding jeep
Sticks in the mud and must be left behind.
An engineer is murdered in his sleep.
The bishop owns a gun, owns up, is fined.
The other engineer begins to weep
And finally admits he's changed his mind.

'So soon !' the bishop cries, 'Come off it, Keith.
It's several hours too early to be scared.
The breasts are all behind us and the see-th-
rough skirts long past, their trials and dangers dared.'
(Up flies the kingfisher. It bares its teeth,
With orange laughter lines and nostrils flared.
Its long crow's feet are spreading out beneath.)
'I would have stayed if I had thought you cared.

'I would have been the party's life and soul,
But all you wanted was a bed of nails.
I would have chopped the logs and fetched the coal,
But all you lived on was the light that fails.
I would have muscled in with bone-and-roll,
But all your victuals came from fagged-out quails.
You trundle on and fossick out your goal.
But as for me, I'm through. I've furled my sails.'

His LEM is waiting at the station
To take him to the mountains of the moon.
On board he hears the countdown with elation,
Is horrified to see his mother swoon
And turn into a dim, distant relation.
He sees his world become a macaroon.
'Quite a small step for our civilisation –
Not at all bad for a legless baboon.'

We track the craft with cynical defiance,
Raising our damp proboscises to sniff
At such a flight, such pitiful reliance
Upon the parabolic hippogriff.
The module vanishes. Blinded by science.
We camp along the edges of the cliff.
Who slip between the sheets at night with giants
Will wake to pillow dew and morning stiff.

Under the glass dome all its feather wilt.
The kingfisher grows tetchy and looks bored.
Beneath the cliffs the dawn spreads miles of silt
And lug-worm castings where the breakers roared
Last night. The tattooed man beneath his quilt
Fondles his tattooed limbs. The cutter's hoard
Supports his head, locked in its custom-built
Toledo-steel-bound chest. He grasps his sword.

All fast asleep. The kingfisher and I
Exchange a soulful look, thinking of Home.
The shovellers home shrieking through the sky.
The kingfisher coughs twice and shakes its comb.
'Don't bite your nails so !' But the bird is sly,
Stares at the red horizon where the foam
Curls like a lip, and weeps : 'Ah, let us fly !'
Nettled, I raise my arm – and break the dome.

Lullaby for a Summer Recess

'Something comes crawling from St James's Park,
Dragging its dripping flippers through the street
With lengths of pondweed trailing from its feet.
It cracks its knuckles in the gathering dark.

'A Human shadow is the only mark
On walls where this and the nightwatchmen meet.
Oh mother, shield my eyeballs from the heat !
It's coming for me. I can hear it bark.'

'Hush child, here come the army in their jeeps,
The nice barbed wire and the barricades.
Your evil godfather takes out his pad.

'The 1922 Committee sleeps
And pallid faces, mooning from the shades,
Are smiling on the kingdom of the sad.'

The Wild Ones

Here come the capybaras on their bikes.
They swerve into the friendly, leafy square
Knocking the angwantibos off their trikes,
Giving the old-age coypus a bad scare.
They specialise in nasty, lightning strikes.
They leave the banks and grocers' shops quite bare,
Then swagger through the bardoors for a shot
Of anything the barman hasn't got.

They spoil the friendly rodent rodeos
By rustling the grazing flocks of mice.
They wear enormous jackboots on their toes.
Insulted by a comment, in a trice
They whip their switchblades out beneath your nose.
Their favourite food is elephant and rice.
Their personal appearance is revolting.
Their fur is never brushed and always moulting.

And in the evening when the sun goes down
They take the comely women in their backs
And ride for several furlongs out of town
Along the muddy roads and mountain tracks,
Wearing a grim and terrifying frown.
Months later, all the females have attacks
And call the coypu doctors to their beds.
What's born has dreadful capybara heads.

Lollipops of the Pomeranian Baroque

The skies remind you of those mounds of custard
Tylman de Gameren so loved to scoff,
With loads of capercaillies, fully busted,
And soft asparaguses to suck off.

The richest, loving earth cow ever manked on
Is there to burden down your dreadful shoes.
But where are all the men? They've turned to plankton,
Or are departing on a winter cruise.

Then are these nuisances really so pesky?
Even the poor mazurka in the snow.
Enough of that! If I was John Sobieskie,
I'd tell those rich Cachoubians where to go.

This Octopus Exploits Women

Even the barnacle has certain rights
The grim anemones should not ignore,
And the gay bivalves in their fishnet tights
Are linking arms with fins to ask for maw.

The hectic round of rockpools is disrupted
By the addresses of the finny vicars,
With which the limpet choirboys were corrupted.
The knitting-fish produce their eight-leg knickers

While somewhere in the depths a voice keeps shouting :
'By Jove! that was a narrow bathyscaphe.'
What made the Junior Sea-Slugs give up scouting?
The *Daily Seaweed* tells us nowhere's safe.

Beneath the shimmering surface of the ocean,
The thoroughfare of ketches, sloops and luggers,
With their thick boots and hair smothered in lotion,
Are gathering hordes of ruthless ichthic muggers.

The workers on the derricks live in terror.
You can't stroll out across the sea at night.
Professor Walrus writes (see *Drowned in Error*) :
'The lemon sole are taught to shoot on sight.'

The lobsters at the water polo club
Sip their prawn cocktails, chatting over chukkas.
The octopus rests idly in its tub.
The Tunny Girls are lounging on its suckers.

Tauler

'If I were a king and did not know it,
   I should be no king ;
But if I was fully convinced that I was a king,
And if all men deemed me so, and further
If I knew that all men deemed me such,
   I should be a king,
And all the riches of the king should be mine.'

In other words, if a king loses confidence,
Logically he must cease to exist.
Much the same is true of gods.
Kings and gods are nowadays much missed.

Tauler, whose words I was quoting,
Himself remarks on good authority :
'The eye by which I see God
Is the same eye by which God sees me.'

God, A Poem

A nasty surprise in a sandwich,
A drawing-pin caught in your sock,
The limpest of shakes from a hand which
You'd thought would be firm as a rock,

A serious mistake in a nightie,
A grave disappointment all round
Is all that you'll get from th'Almighty,
Is all that you'll get underground.

Oh he *said*: 'If you lay off the crumpet
I'll see you alright in the end.
Just hang on until the last trumpet.
Have faith in me, chum – I'm your friend.'

But if you remind him, he'll tell you:
'I'm sorry, I must have been pissed –
Though your name rings a sort of a bell. You
Should have guessed that I do not exist.

'I didn't exist at Creation,
I didn't exist at the Flood,
And I won't be around for Salvation
To sort out the sheep from the cud –

'Or whatever the phrase is. The fact is
In soteriological terms
I'm a crude existential malpractice
And you are a diet of worms.

'You're a nasty surprise in a sandwich.
You're a drawing-pin caught in my sock.
You're the limpest of shakes from a hand which
I'd have thought would be firm as a rock,

'You're a serious mistake in a nightie,
You're a grave disappointment all round –
That's all that you are,' says th'Almighty,
'And that's all that you'll be underground.'

VII

Songs

Nothing

I take a jewel from a junk-shop tray
And wish I had a love to buy it for.
Nothing I choose will make you turn my way.
Nothing I give will make you love me more.

I know that I've embarrassed you too long
And I'm ashamed to linger at your door.
Whatever I embark on will be wrong.
Nothing I do will make you love me more.

I cannot work. I cannot read or write.
How can I frame a letter to implore.
Eloquence is a lie. The truth is trite.
Nothing I say will make you love me more.

So I replace the jewel in the tray
And laughingly pretend I'm far too poor.
Nothing I give, nothing I do or say,
Nothing I am will make you love me more.

The Song That Sounds Like This
To Philip Dennis

Have you not heard the song
The Song That Sounds Like This
When skies are overcast and looks grow long
And Radio Three
Is all your tea-time company.
The last of the first infusion comes so strong
The apostle spoon wakes up
And clambers from the cup.
Have you not heard it? Have you not heard the song –
Antithesis of bliss –
The Song That Sounds Like This!

Have you not heard them sing
Those songs that sound like these
When yearning for the telephone to ring.
The sky is dark.
The dogs have gone to foul the park.
The first of the next infusion tastes like string.
Oh melancholy sound.
All the apostle spoons have drowned.
Have you not heard them, have you not heard them sing –
No more, oh please,
Oh give us no more songs,
Oh give us no more Songs That Sound Like These!

The Killer Snails

The killer snails
Have slung their silver trails
Along the doormat, out across the lawn,
Under the bushes
Where the alarming thrushes
Give night its notice, making way for dawn,
And the obliging lizards drop their tails.

On webs of dew
The spiders stir their pots of glue
And drag their quartered victims to the shade.
Soaked in their rugs
Of grass and moss the slugs
Wind up another night of sluggish trade
And young ingredients get into a stew.

The sorrel bends.
The path fades out but never ends
Where brambles clutch and bracken wipes your feet.
It goes in rings.
Its mind's on other things.
Its way and its intentions never meet.
Meetings of friends?
It gives no undertaking. It depends.

Notes & Acknowledgements

DEAD SOLDIERS

Cambodia 1973. The APCs (armoured personnel carriers) are mounted with recoilless rifles. The prince is military governor of Kompong Speu province.

CHOSUN

Material drawn from the turn-of-the-century magazine *The Korean Repository*, *A History of Korean Alphabet and Movable Types* by Shin Bumshik (Seoul, 1970), *Undiplomatic Memories* by William Franklin Sands (London, n.d.), and in particular from *Korean Patterns* by Paul S. Crane (Seoul, 4th ed. 1978).

EXEMPLA

1. Found in J. Y. Lettvin *et al.* : 'What the Frog's Eye tells the Frog's Brain'. (*Proc. Inst. Radio. Engrs. N.Y.* 1940)
2. Found.
3. & 4. From *Mycologia*, Vol. 60.
5. Found in Pitt-Rivers Museum, Oxford.
6. Oxford billboard, 1968.
7. Found in Smith and Miller's *Developmental Psycholinguistics*.
8. Found in Pitt-Rivers Museum, Oxford.
9. Found in Smith and Miller's *Developmental Psycholinguistics*.
10. Found in Pitt-Rivers Museum, Oxford.
11. Found in *The Fruit-Grower* by Raymond Bush (Penguin Books Ltd).
12. Lyell, *Principles of Geology*.
A. From museum labels.
B. Italicised passages from Raymond Bush, op. cit.
C. *vide* Exempla 3 and 4.
D. *vide* Exemplum 12.

About the Author

JAMES FENTON was born in Lincoln, England, in 1949. He was educated at Magdalen College, Oxford, where he won the Newdigate Prize for Poetry. He has worked as a political and literary journalist on the *New Statesman*, was a freelance reporter in Indochina, and spent a year in Germany working for the *Guardian*. He is now theater critic for the *London Sunday Times*.

Fenton's first collection of poems, *Terminal Moraine*, was published in London in 1972. His collected poems to date, *The Memory of War*, appeared in 1982. The Random House edition of Fenton's work includes all the poems in *The Memory of War*, as well as those published in the pamphlet *Children in Exile*, which appeared in Britain in 1983.